VW Beetle

Tracy Maurer

Rourke
Publishing LLC
Vero Beach, Florida 32964

www.rourkepublishing.com

AUTHOR CREDITS:
The author gratefully acknowledges project assistance provided by Michael Leander and the team at Denny Hecker's Auto Connection in Inver Grove Heights, MN. Also, the author extends appreciation to Sean Wagner, Mike Maurer, Lois M. Nelson, Margaret and Thomas.

PHOTO CREDITS: Courtesy of DaimlerChrysler: page 5 (inset); Courtesy of Ford Motor Company: page 6; Courtesy of Volkswagen: all others

Editor: Robert Stengard-Olliges
Cover Design: Todd Field
Page Design: Nicola Stratford

Library of Congress Cataloging-in-Publication Data

Maurer, Tracy, 1965-
 VW Beetle : full throttle / Tracy Nelson Maurer.
   p. cm. -- (Full throttle)
 Includes index.
 ISBN 1-60044-229-3 (hardcover)
 ISBN 978-1-60044-369-5 (paperback)
 1. Volkswagen Beetle automobile--Juvenile literature. 2. Volkswagen New Beetle automobile--Juvenile literature. I. Title. II. Series: Maurer, Tracy, 1965-. Full throttle
 TL215.V6M375 2007
 629.222'2--dc22

                       2006017832

Printed in the USA

CG/CG

Rourke Publishing

www.rourkepublishing.com – sales@rourkepublishing.com
Post Office Box 3328, Vero Beach, FL 32964

Table of Contents

Type 1 Time

For more than sixty years, Volkswagen (VW) sold the original Beetle without any big changes to its basic little car. The German company made tweaks here and there—some 78,000 improvements over time—but the Beetle was still the same reliable, affordable, and easy-to fix car as always.

America's safety and emissions laws stopped Beetles from coming into the U.S. after 1978. But the VW factory in Mexico was still building the original model when the New Beetle took the motoring world by surprise in 1998.

Back in the 1920s, only wealthy people could afford automobiles. **Nazi** leader Adolf Hitler wanted Germany to build a low-cost "kleinauto" (small car) for workers to drive. He ordered Ferdinand Porsche (yes, *that* Porsche racecar designer) to create a low-cost vehicle.

Jewish motoring editor Joseph Ganz drew up designs for a rear-mounted engine in a small car long before Hitler rose to power in the 1930s. Ganz, and probably others like him, never received official recognition for their part in motoring history.

The Beetle shape is an icon or image recognized worldwide, just like Mickey Mouse ears and the Coca-Cola bottle.

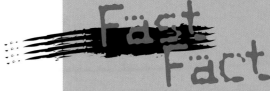

Fast Fact

Ferdinand Porsche used the term "Volkswagen" for his small car. It means "peoples' car."

Hans Ledwinka designed the 1934 Czechoslovakian Tatra T77 with an air-cooled, rear-mounted engine that probably inspired Porsche's work on the Volkswagen. American Chrysler Airflows and Lincoln-Zephyrs may have offered a few ideas, too.

First Volkswagen Design Demands:

- Fit a family of five
- Air-cooled engine
- Fuel economy of 40 miles per gallon (mpg)
- Capable of cruising at 62 miles (100 km) per hour
- Cost less than half the price of most small cars then

Just ten years after re-opening, the Wolfsburg factory built its one millionth VW.

German Nazis built a huge factory at Wolfsburg to make Volkswagens (VWs). World War II started in 1939 before any cars rolled out. The plant switched to building military vehicles instead. Slave labor produced Porsche's Kübelwagen (a failed attempt at a Jeep) and the Schwimmwagen to travel on land and in the water.

After the war ended in 1945, the British helped clean up the bombed-out factory to start building Type 1 cars. Later called Beetles, Type 1s were produced there until 1974.

Hitler admired the Ford Model T. He used Henry Ford's pre-payment idea to make German workers put money into an account to buy their Volkswagens. Unlike Ford's plan, the Nazi program never delivered any vehicles. The workers lost their savings.

cabriolet
a car with a fold-down
top; a convertible

ORIGINAL BEETLE MILESTONES

1936 Ferdinand Porsche tested three
Type 1 prototypes.
1944 Allies bombed the Wolfsburg plant.
1945 Britain helped the VW plant produce
the Type 1.
1949 VW introduced Karmann **Cabriolets,**
four-seater convertibles.
1978 The last Beetles sent to the U.S. for sale.
1994 The New Beetle "Concept 1" unveiled
at Detroit Auto Show.
2003 Mexico's factory made the very last
original Beetle.

Fast Fact

Until 1953, the Type 1
had a split rear window
and a push-button starter
on the dash.

Original Beetles could float.
Really! Researchers tested
one that bobbed for more
than 40 minutes. Many
Beetle drivers swear their
cars saved them from
drowning in flash floods.

Beetlemania!

"Beetlemania" and "Beatlemania" hit the United States in the 1960s. Younger Americans, called **baby boomers**, loved both European imports—the Beetle cars and the Beatles band. The car was everywhere "old" people weren't.

Boomer Rebels

The gas-sipping little Beetle made a rebel statement next to a parental gas-guzzling land-yacht. Unlike American cars, the German Beetles were small and simple.

Boomer College Students

The Beetle was affordable and easy to fix. The car proved popular on campuses for contests to see how many students could stuff into one.

Boomer Surfers

Rear-wheel-drive Beetles drove well over the sand, perfect for the beach scene.

Boomer Hippies

Hippies painted their Beetles with slogans, flowers, and other art. They drove them to rock concerts, war protests, and folk festivals.

The Beetle became an icon, or symbol, of the 1960s.

Warm-weather states like California owned more Beetles than cold-weather states. The original Bug's air-cooled engines never put out enough heat to thaw northern owners.

baby boomers
the large generation of people born after World War II, generally from 1946 to 1964

hippies
rebel youth of the 1960s and 1970s who generally opposed traditional views

Fast Fact

Americans bought 423,000 Beetles in 1968—the most VWs ever in one year.

Sturdy Car, Silly Name

The original Volkswagen started simply as Type 1. Nazis tried to call it the "Kraft durch Freude (KdF) Wagen." It meant "strength through joy" to promote one of Hitler's shady programs. After the war, the public nicknamed the little car "Beetle" and it stuck. Around the world, the name translated into names for a bug, hunchback, turtle, snail, and bellybutton (because everyone has one).

Why "Beetle"?

- Small, bug-like shape
- Buzzing engine sound
- Lots and lots of them
- Travels anywhere and everywhere
- Slow but steady

Volkswagen finally dropped the Type 1 name in 1968 and called it a "Beetle."

10

Volkswagen become Europe's largest carmaker by selling Golf and Polo cars—not by selling Beetles. Some Volkswagen managers saw the original Beetle as a sorry reminder of World War II's dark days. Others thought the Beetle was simply outdated. Few realized how deeply Americans loved the 1960s icon.

Beetlemania Again

The New Beetle didn't have a world war hanging over it as the first Beetle did. But, in the late 1980s, Volkswagen was certainly losing the battle for American car buyers. New Beetles had plenty of competition, including the Dodge Neon introduced the same year with round "Beetle-like" features.

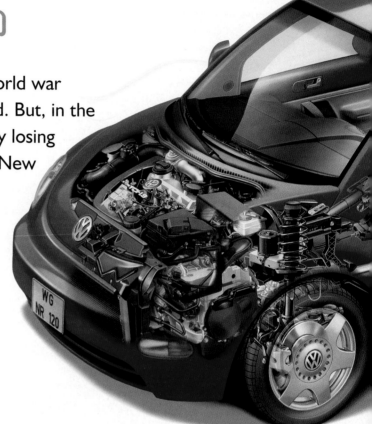

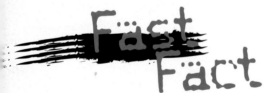

The top-secret Beetle project was code-named "Lightning Bug" and included ideas for using an electric engine.

A creative team in California secretly drew plans for an all-new Beetle to fire up lagging American sales. The team worked for three years to create a unique car that would convince VW's German managers to OK its production—and to develop a car that tapped Americans' love for the original Beetle.

Concept 1, later called the New Beetle, used the very compact VW Polo chassis. The production version grew from there.

NEW BEETLE MILESTONES

1991 J. Mays and Freeman Thomas secretly drew ideas for a New Beetle.

1994 VW unveiled the "Concept 1" at the Detroit Auto Show.

1995 Positive response prompted VW to move the Concept 1 into production.

1996 VW used the "New Beetle" name for its convertible at the Geneva Auto Show.

1997 New Beetles rolled into U.S. dealerships.

2003 The convertible option became available for the New Beetle.

2006 VW redesigned the New Beetle—and it's still a cute Bug.

To show its forward thinking, VW offered live Internet chats with the Beetle design center when it unveiled the New Beetle at the Geneva Auto Show in 1996. Back then, e-mail and the World Wide Web were barely hatched.

Fresh Memories

The designers updated the famous three-bubble shape. The New Beetle had to quickly remind people of the original Beetle, but with a fresh look. The VW team wanted the car to look cute but not silly. It had to offer solid safety features and deliver an entirely modern driving experience.

The New Beetle seems to smile coming or going. Two round headlights in front and two round taillights in back look like eyes. The curvy hood and curvy trunk form a happy smile. A centered VW badge makes the nose on each end. The pudgy fenders add to its hug-a bug appeal.

The VW badge on the trunk cleverly hides the latch for the rear hatch.

The New Beetle designers echoed the car's round shape by using circles in many other parts of the car. The side windows formed a large arc. Tinted glass and a black support bar between the front and rear windows emphasized the semi-circle shape.

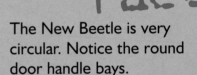

The New Beetle is very circular. Notice the round door handle bays.

The circle theme continued on the inside. The designers set the circular dashboard gauges behind the three-spoked steering wheel as on the original Beetle.

Convertible Bug

The biggest news for the two-door New Beetle came in 2003 when Volkswagen unveiled a convertible body style. Karmann, a famous car-body design firm, created the new option. Karmann also built the Cabriolet for the original Beetle. The New Beetle convertible added an automatic pop-up roll bar for added safety and an optional power roof.

More Choices

Today, Beetle buyers can choose a hatchback or convertible. Standard features include air conditioning; power windows, locks and mirrors; cruise control; seat-height adjusters; and adjustable steering wheel. Volkswagen has added more deluxe options, too:

- 17-inch (43 cm) wheels
- Leather upholstery
- CD changer
- Satellite radio
- Sunroof on hatchbacks or a power top on convertibles

MP3 Ports

Research showed that online music buyers were more than twice as likely to own a Volkswagen than the average Internet users. Now New Beetles have MP3 ports in the dash to appeal to that market.

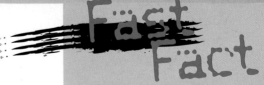

Fast Fact

A driver can raise or lower the convertible's power roof in just 13 seconds.

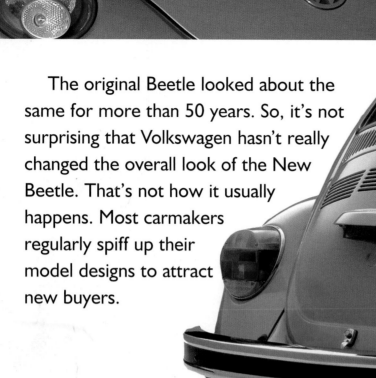

The original Beetle looked about the same for more than 50 years. So, it's not surprising that Volkswagen hasn't really changed the overall look of the New Beetle. That's not how it usually happens. Most carmakers regularly spiff up their model designs to attract new buyers.

Fast Fact

Volkswagen of America, Inc. (VWoA), has operated as a **subsidiary** and sole U.S. importer of cars manufactured by Volkswagen AG (VWAG) for more than 50 years.

WHAT'S OLD? (1967 Beetle)

- Rear engine
- Noisy buzzing sound
- Horizontally opposed boxer 4-cylinder
- Air cooled
- From 35 to 55 horsepower
- 0 to 60 miles (97 km) per hour in 4 weeks (OK, maybe it just seemed that slow)
- **Rear-wheel drive**
- No-nonsense interior
- 1,790 pounds (3,938 kg) curb weight
- Engine in back, trunk in front

front-wheel drive
    a system that sends the engine's power to the front wheels, which pull the car forward and steer

rear-wheel drive
    the engine drives the rear wheels, pushing the vehicle forward

subsidiary
    operating separately but to benefit another group or person, usually the owner

WHAT'S NEW? (2006 Beetle)

- Front engine
- Quiet purr
- Inline 5-cylinder or 4-cylinder turbo diesel
- Liquid (water) cooled
- Up to 150 horsepower
- 0 to 60 miles (97 km) per hour in as little as 8.4 seconds
- **Front-wheel drive**
- Comfortable interior with CD player, air bags, air conditioning, power windows and heat
- 2,712 pounds (5,966 kg) curb weight
- Engine in front, trunk in back

Style Changes in 2006

- Bolder front and rear bumpers
- More oval-shaped headlights and taillights
- Updated gauges with chrome accents
- Dual driver sun visors

19

Safer and Faster

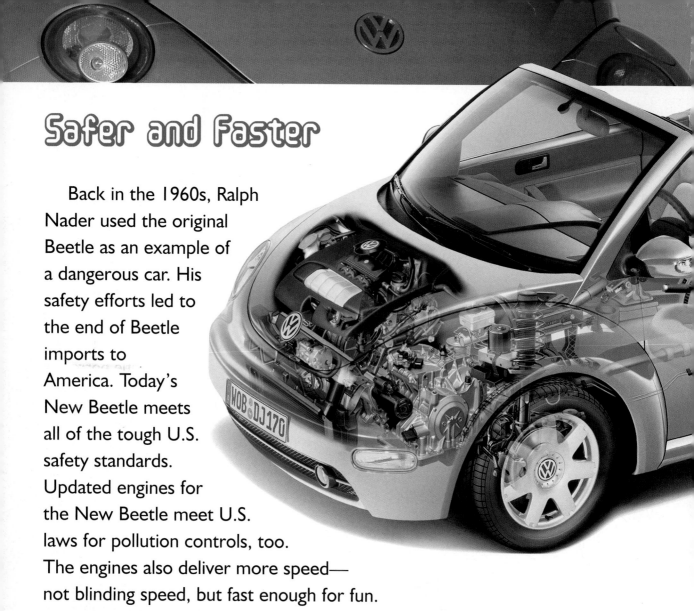

Back in the 1960s, Ralph Nader used the original Beetle as an example of a dangerous car. His safety efforts led to the end of Beetle imports to America. Today's New Beetle meets all of the tough U.S. safety standards. Updated engines for the New Beetle meet U.S. laws for pollution controls, too. The engines also deliver more speed—not blinding speed, but fast enough for fun.

Crash Test

U.S. Insurance Institute for Highway Safety (IIHS) tests showed that the 2006 Volkswagen New Beetle protected passengers very well in 40 mile (64 km) per hour **offset** front-end crashes.

ESP

The Electronic Stabilization Program (ESP) delivers traction control. This standard feature improved the New Beetle's handling and stability.

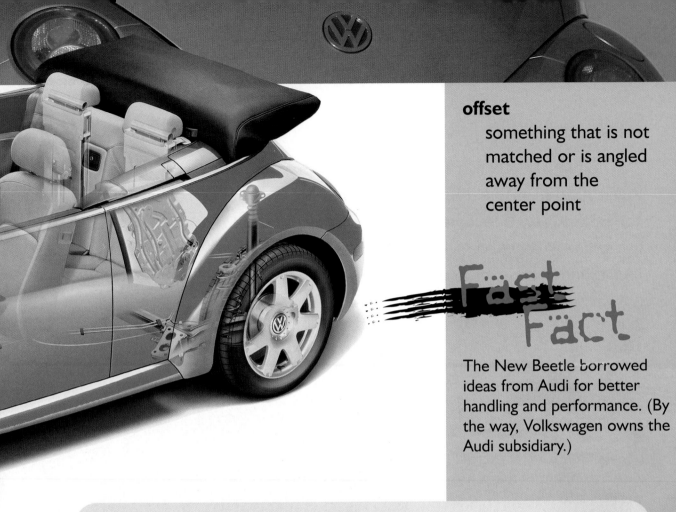

offset
> something that is not matched or is angled away from the center point

Fast Fact

The New Beetle borrowed ideas from Audi for better handling and performance. (By the way, Volkswagen owns the Audi subsidiary.)

Ferdinand Piëch, the VW chairman, expected more than clever design and better safety features in the New Beetle. He demanded that it also deliver a smooth, high-quality, and enjoyable driving experience or VW would not sell the model.

Ready to Cruise

The New Beetle first hit the market with an inline four-**cylinder** engine. More powerful engines soon followed. Today, the New Beetle hatchback comes with a 2.5-liter, five-cylinder engine or a 1.9-liter **turbo-charged** four-cylinder diesel engine. The New Beetle convertible is only available with a 2.5-liter gasoline engine.

Liter, as in a 2.5-liter engine, is a measurement of the engine's size.

Volkswagen's clever Direct Shift Gearbox (DSG) **transmission** for the diesel motor works like an automatic transmission without a clutch. The computer controls the six-speed shifting. Drivers can opt to shift manually, too.

The New Beetle hatchback diesel can stretch its fuel economy to more than 40 miles to the gallon.

The gasoline motor can deliver about 30 miles to the gallon— better than many cars.

cylinder
    in motors, a chamber where the fuel is burned
transmission
    in vehicles, the unit of gears that allows the engine's power to move the wheels
turbo-charged
    a vehicle using a special fan turned by the engine's exhaust gases that works to pump more air into the cylinders and boost power output

The New Beetle's standard 2.5-liter engine purrs with 150 horsepower. The fresh-paced engine first appeared on the Jetta, a popular Volkswagen model. A five-speed manual or a six-speed automatic transmission sends power to the front-wheel-drive system.

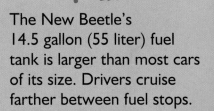

Fast Fact

The New Beetle's 14.5 gallon (55 liter) fuel tank is larger than most cars of its size. Drivers cruise farther between fuel stops.

The Past in the Present

Much of the New Beetle's success links into the original Beetle's past. The two models often share the spotlight even today. Cute and friendly as the original, the New Beetle is instantly recognizable as a Beetle. Yet, they're very different vehicles. The New Beetle is unique—just as the California designers imagined.

For a while, original Beetles were built on one side of the Volkswagen factory in Puebla, Mexico, while New Beetles were built on the other side.

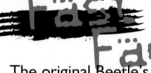

The original Beetle's final production count in 2003 totaled over 21,500,000. It easily broke Ford's Model T production record of 15 million vehicles. The New Beetle won't pass either record.

The Puebla factory made the last original Beetles on July 30, 2003.

All New Beetles that arrive in the U.S. come from Puebla, Mexico. In less than three hours, a painted New Beetle body joins the rest of its parts to make a complete car.

The original Beetles sold worldwide. Today, Mexico probably has the most of any nation—some two million cars. Many Beetles there served as taxicabs until the country set strict air pollution limits and safety laws.

Legendary Ties

As the chairman of Volkswagen, Ferdinand Piëch approved production of the New Beetle. Nearly 70 years earlier, Ferdinand Porsche, his grandfather, developed the first Beetle.

The original Beetle later inspired the Porsche 356. The Porsche 356 influenced the Audi TT or "A" platform—which is also the New Beetle's platform (and the Golf's).

Disney released its blockbuster hit, Herbie, the Love Bug, in 1969. Three sequels followed, plus a short TV run. In 2005, Herbie, Fully Loaded brought the classic up to NASCAR speed. Herbie, an original Beetle, falls in love with a flirty New Beetle.

In the 2005 movie Herbie, Fully Loaded, Maggie bought Herbie for $75—the same price paid in the 1969 movie.

Fun with Bugs

People love their Bugs—original or New Beetle models. They gather at VW shows all over the world. One of the largest events started in 1987 in the United Kingdom. Today, Bug Jam brings Beetle fans together from all over the world to share stories, swap parts, and run the Santa Pod Raceway.

The Volkswagen Drag Racing Club in England hosts competitions for modified Bugs. Most of the cars started as original Beetles. The New Beetle will probably find its way to the racing scene someday, too.

Today, the original Beetle has become popular for the wild off-road courses in the Baja desert of Mexico. Drivers modify their original Beetles with bigger wheels and tires to handle the rugged terrain.

In America, it's easy to spot both the original Beetles and New Beetles. It's so easy that kids invented a game for it. Called Punch Buggy or Slug Bug, the game started more than thirty years ago with the original Beetle. Today, Slug Bug now includes spotting the New Beetle, too. There's no national championship. There are no points and no judges. Although some Websites list complex rules, it's just fun—like Beetles!

Few cars have had the long success and global appeal as the Beetle. Nobody plays Corvette games. No other car has starred in two generations of hit movies. While the New Beetle might not break the original production record, it has certainly found its place in motoring history.

How to Play Slug Bug

The game starts with at least two players, most often riding in the backseat of the same car. When a kid sees a Beetle, he or she "calls" it by (gently!) punching all other players. The puncher must say, "Slug Bug, yellow (or whatever color it is) Bug, no back." If the caller doesn't say the color or "no back," then the other players can punch the caller. That's it!

Glossary

baby boomers (BAY bee BOOM urz) – the large generation of people born after World War II, generally from 1946 to 1964

cabriolet (CAB ree ah LAY) – a car with a fold-down top; a convertible

cylinder (SILL in dur) – in motors, a chamber where the fuel is burned to create pressure

front-wheel drive (FRUNT WEEL DRIHV) – a system that sends the engine's power to the front wheels, which pull the car forward and steer

hippies (HIP eez) – rebel youth of the 1960s and 1970s who generally opposed traditional views

Nazi (NAHT see) – refers to the National Socialist German Workers Party of Germany, especially from 1933 to 1945

offset (OFF set) – something that is not matched or is angled away from the center point

rear-wheel drive (REER WEEL DRIHV) – the engine drives the rear wheels, pushing the vehicle forward

subsidiary (sub SID ee ahr ee) – operating separately but to benefit another group or person, usually the owner

transmission (trans MISH un) – in vehicles, the unit of gears that allows the engine's power to move the wheels

turbo-charged (TUR boh charjd) – a vehicle using a special fan turned by the engine's exhaust gases that works to pump more air into the cylinders and boost power output

Further Reading

Cheetham, Craig ed. *Hot Cars of the 60s: The Best Cars from Around the World*. Advanced Global Distribution, 2004.

Copping, Richard and Cservenka, Ken. *Volkswagen Beetle: The Essential Buyer's Guide*. Veloce Publishing, 2005.

Hale, James. *Dune Buggies*. MBI Publishing, 2004.

Websites

www.bugjam.co.uk

www.newbeetle.org

www.vvwca.com

www.vw.com

Index

About the Author

Tracy Nelson Maurer writes nonfiction and fiction books for children, including more than 50 titles for Rourke Publishing LLC. Tracy lives with her husband Mike and two children near Minneapolis, Minnesota.

5/07